SEAWEED SOUP

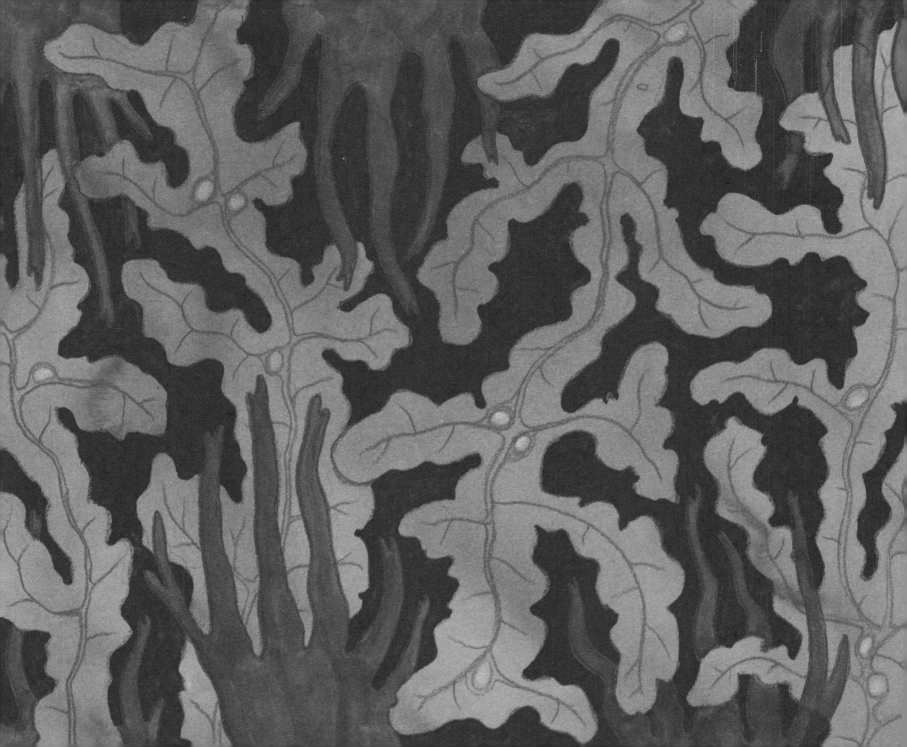

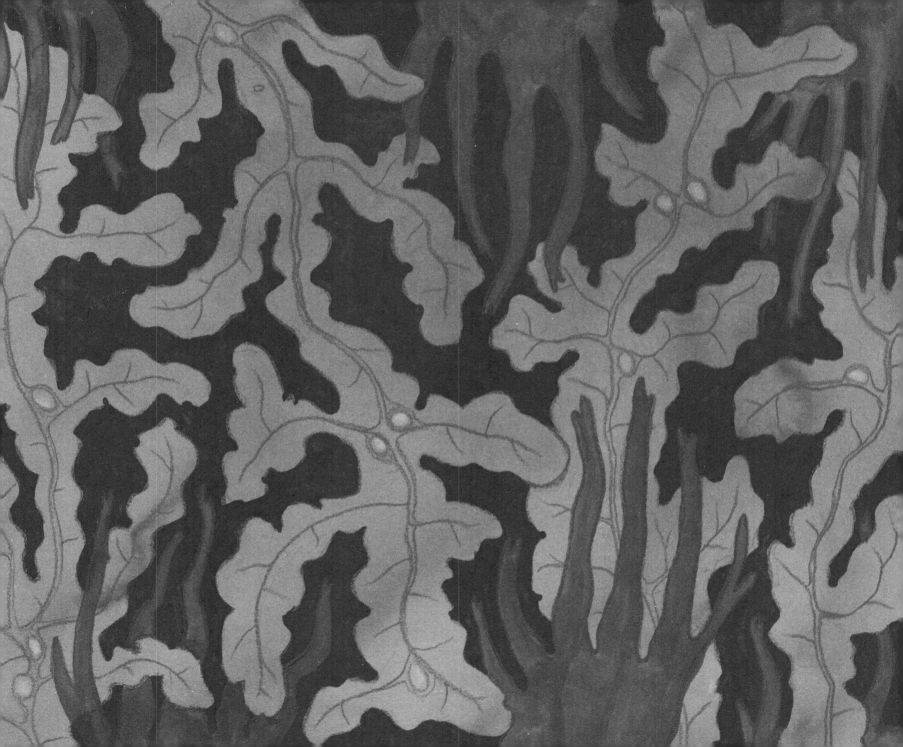

SEAWEED SOUP

by Stuart J. Murphy • illustrated by Frank Remkiewicz

SCHOLASTIC INC.
New York Toronto London Auckland Sydney
Mexico City New Delhi Hong Kong Buenos Aires

*To Sarah Thomson—who blends her great ideas and
wonderful insights to make the perfect MathStart soup
—S.J.M.*

*For Dick and Linda Shute: great soup-makers
—F.R.*

The publisher and author would like to thank teachers Patricia Chase, Phyllis Goldman,
and Patrick Hopfensperger for their help in making the math in MathStart just right for kids.

ISBN 0-439-46116-2

12 11 10 9 8 7 6 5 4 3 2   6 7 8/0

Printed in the U.S.A.   08

First Scholastic printing, May 2003

Typography by Elynn Cohen

MathStart® is a registered trademark of HarperCollins Publishers.

Bugs incorporated in the MathStart series design were painted by Jon Buller.

Seaweed Soup

One day Turtle decided to make seaweed soup. He stirred and he stirred until it was perfect—thick and green, gooey and slimy. Turtle couldn't wait to have lunch.

He put 4 things on the table—a bright red cup for gooseberry juice, a great big spoon, a napkin, and one of his nicest bowls.

Turtle was just about to fill his bowl when along came his friend Crab.

"Would you like to join me for lunch?" asked Turtle. "I just made a pot of seaweed soup."

"Yuck," thought Crab. "It's green! It's slimy! And it's *smelly*! But how can I say no to a friend?"

"Take my place and I'll get another cup, spoon, napkin, and bowl for myself," said Turtle.

He had 3 of the things he needed to make a complete set, but he couldn't find another cup. "Well, this glass will have to do," he said.

Turtle came back to the table with a glass instead of a cup, another big spoon, another napkin, and another nice bowl. He was about to pour the gooseberry juice when Sandpiper and Seagull came flapping along.

"There's a pot of something icky next to Turtle's table," piped Sandpiper.

"And it smells awful, too," squawked Seagull. "Hurry and fly away before he sees us!"

But Turtle spotted them and yelled out,
"Come and join us for lunch!"

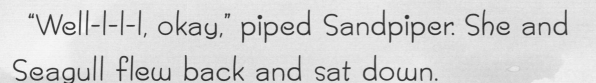

"Well-l-l-l, okay," piped Sandpiper. She and Seagull flew back and sat down.

Turtle said, "One of you can take my place and the other can sit right here while I look for two more complete sets of everything."

Turtle looked all around. There was one glass left but it didn't match, the only bowls left were cracked, and there was only one more big spoon. "Well, these will have to do," he said.

14

After filling the yellow cup and the jelly jar with gooseberry juice and the two cracked bowls with soup, Turtle finally sat down. But just then, Clam poked her head out of the sand.

"What's that smell? Disgusting!" she thought, and started to dig back down.

But Turtle hollered, "Please have lunch with us, Clam. There's plenty of seaweed soup."

Clam thought it would be mean to say no.
"I suppose I can," she gurgled.
  "Take my place," said Turtle.
  He looked for another set, but
there was nothing left—not a
cup or a glass or even a jelly jar,
not a spoon, a napkin, or a bowl
of any kind.

While Turtle was gone, Crab said,
"I guess we'd better try the soup."
"But it's disgusting and slimy,"
complained Sandpiper.
"And smelly and gooey,"
added Seagull.

Clam just shut her eyes and took a little spoonful.

"Wow! It tastes great!"
she gurgled with surprise.
Then Sandpiper tried it.
"Yummy," she piped.
"Delicious," squawked
Seagull.
"Amazing!" said Crab.

They sipped and they slurped until the entire pot of seaweed soup was gone.

Finally, Turtle came back to the table carrying a set of 4 things—a big seashell for a cup, a toy shovel for a spoon, a beach towel for a napkin, and a rusty old pail for a bowl. "These will have to do," he said. "Now let's eat that soup!"

His friends looked
at one another.
Nobody said a word.

At last Clam admitted, "I'm sorry, Turtle, but when you were gone we ate all the seaweed soup."

Without a word, Turtle turned around
and walked off.

"He's mad at us," whispered Seagull.

"What can we do?" asked Crab.

Soon Turtle came back.
He was carrying another pot of soup—
thick and green, gooey and slimy, and
just as smelly as the first one.
And he said, "You can never
make too much seaweed soup!"

REVIEW OF ALL THE SETS

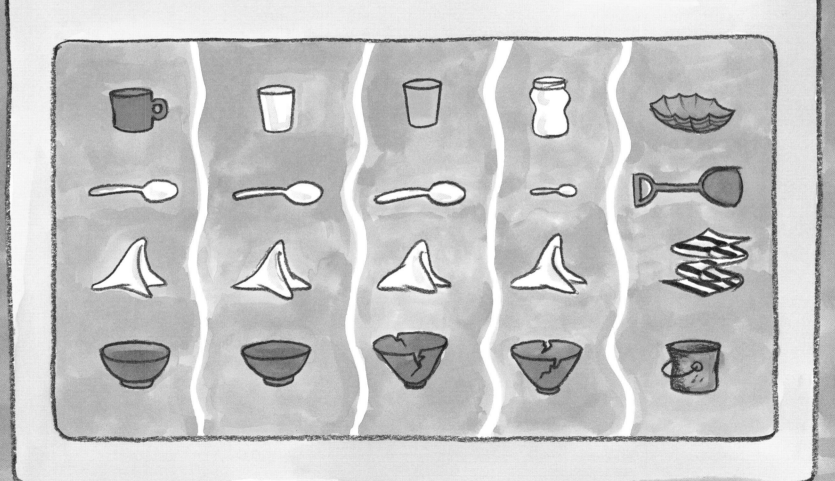

FOR ADULTS AND KIDS

In *Seaweed Soup*, the math concept presented is matching sets, or one-to-one correspondence. Understanding sets is an important step in counting, understanding more than/less than, and learning about patterns and relationships.

If you would like to have more fun with the math concepts presented in *Seaweed Soup*, here are a few suggestions:

• Read the story with the child and describe what is going on in each picture. Ask questions like: "Now how many animals are coming to lunch?" "How is the table setting on this page different from the table setting on the previous page? Why did it change?"

• While reading the story, ask the child what things each new character will need in order to eat lunch. As each new guest arrives, count the number of cups, spoons, napkins, and bowls on the table. Discuss how each guest has 1 cup, 1 spoon, 1 napkin, and 1 bowl.

• Ask the child such questions as: "Suppose there are 8 people coming to the house for dinner and there are only 6 spoons on the table. How many more spoons will we need?" or "Suppose everyone in the family will need 2 spoons for dinner. How many spoons will we need altogether?"

• After reading the story, act it out by setting a table using different types of cups, spoons, napkins, and bowls for each of the 5 characters. After acting out the story, have the child compare the table he or she set to the table at the end of the story.

Following are some activities that will help you extend the concepts presented in *Seaweed Soup* into a child's everyday life:

Lunch Party: Plan a lunch party (real or make-believe) with the child's favorite soup as the main course. Have the child figure out how many cups, spoons, napkins, and bowls will be needed for the lunch.

Around the House: Have the child count the number of spoons, knives, and forks in the kitchen. Is there a spoon for every fork? How many sets of 1 spoon, 1 knife, and 1 fork can you make?

Game: Make two rows of pennies (any number will do) in front of each child. Ask, "Do your sets of pennies match?" Ask the children to close their eyes. Add 1 penny to or take 1 away from some of the rows. When the children open their eyes, ask, "Who has 2 rows that don't match? How can we make them match?" If a child answers correctly, he or she gets 1 penny from each of the other players. Repeat. Whoever ends up with the most pennies wins.

The following stories include concepts similar to those that are presented in *Seaweed Soup*:

- Anno's Math Games II by Mitsumasa Anno

- Hannah and the Seven Dresses by Marthe Jocelyn

- Bread, Bread, Bread by Ann Morris

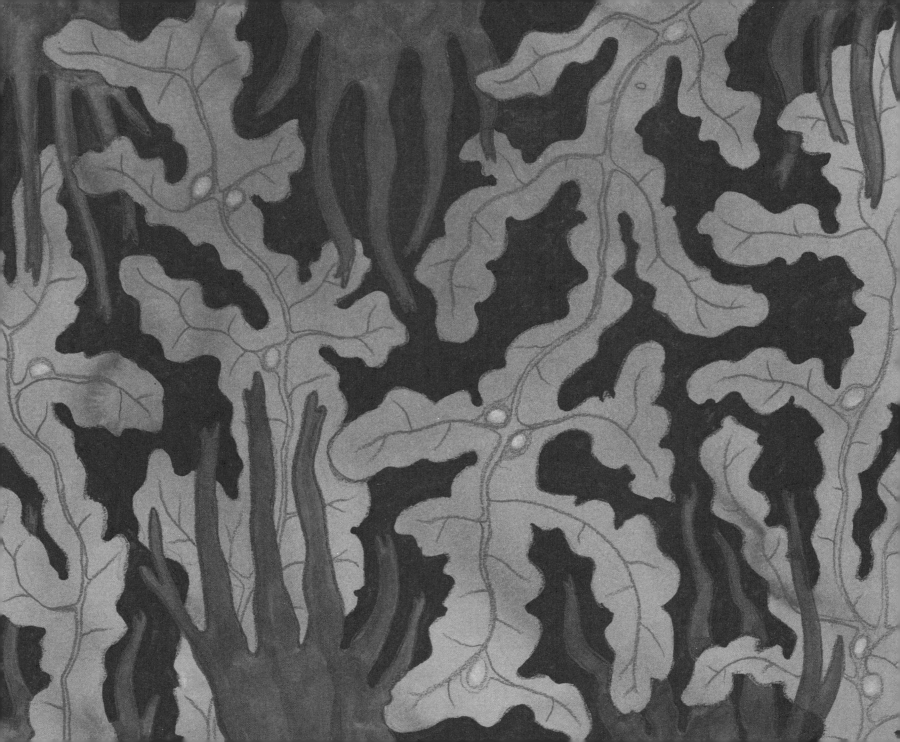

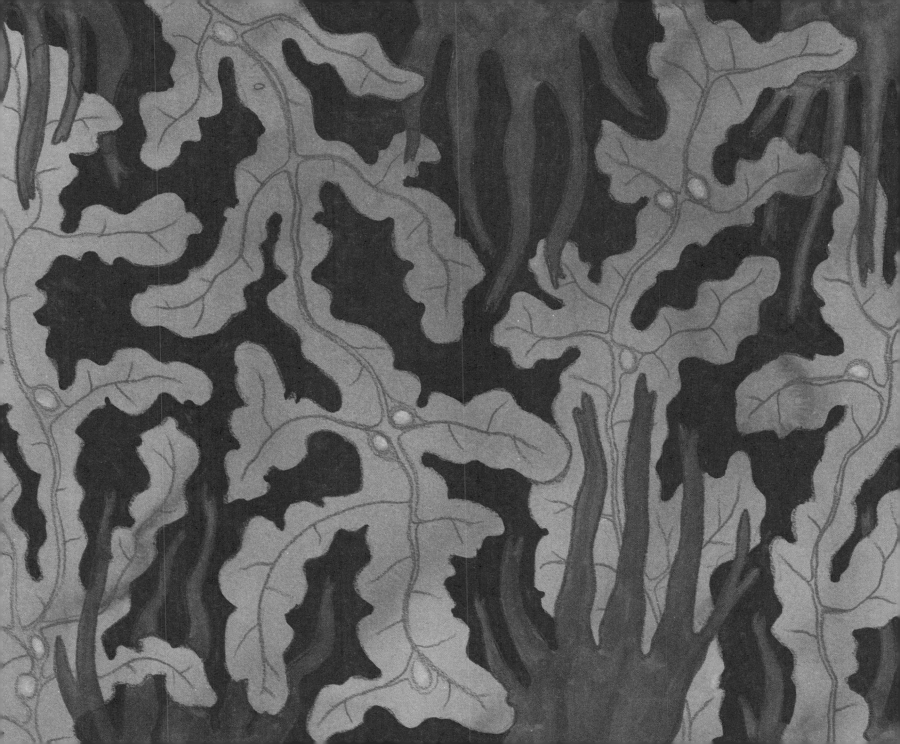

STUART J. MURPHY is a visual learning specialist. A graduate of the Rhode Island School of Design, he has a strong background in design and art direction. He also has extensive experience in the world of educational publishing. Drawing on all these talents, Stuart J. Murphy brings a unique perspective to the **MathStart** series. In **MathStart** books, pictures do more than tell stories; they teach math.

Stuart J. Murphy and his wife, Nancy, live in Evanston, Illinois.

FRANK REMKIEWICZ has illustrated the ever-popular Animal Crackers box, as well as RABBIT'S PAJAMA PARTY and JUST ENOUGH CARROTS in the **MathStart** series. His other books for children include the well-known Froggy series by Jonathan London and the Horrible Harry series by Suzy Kline.

Frank and his family live in Sarasota, Florida.